GREEN PLANET
WIND POWER

by Rebecca Pettiford

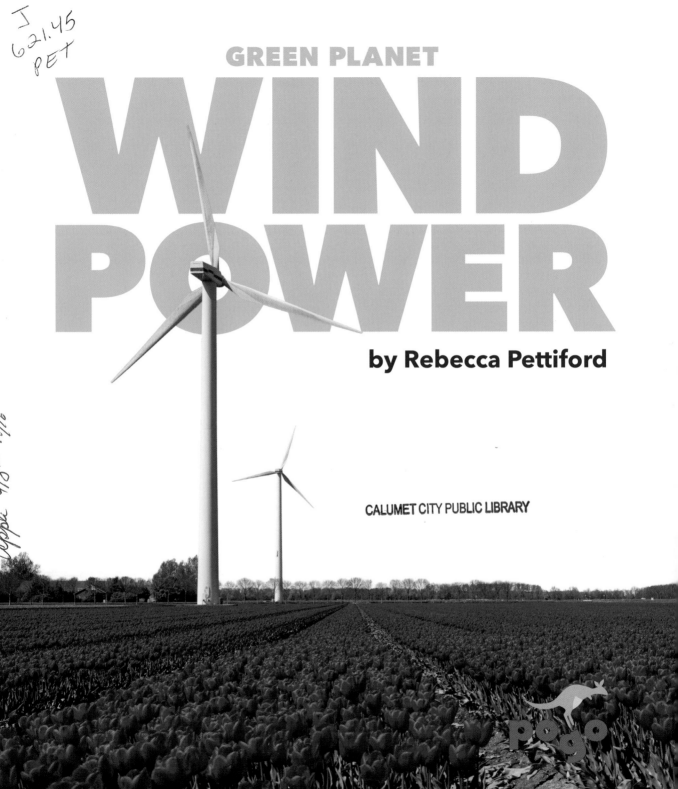

pogo

Ideas for Parents and Teachers

Pogo Books let children practice reading informational text while introducing them to nonfiction features such as headings, labels, sidebars, maps, and diagrams, as well as a table of contents, glossary, and index.

Carefully leveled text with a strong photo match offers early fluent readers the support they need to succeed.

Before Reading

- "Walk" through the book and point out the various nonfiction features. Ask the student what purpose each feature serves.
- Look at the glossary together. Read and discuss the words.

Read the Book

- Have the child read the book independently.
- Invite him or her to list questions that arise from reading.

After Reading

- Discuss the child's questions. Talk about how he or she might find answers to those questions.
- Prompt the child to think more. Ask: Have you ever seen a wind farm? Do you know of any places that get their electricity from wind power?

Pogo Books are published by Jump!
5357 Penn Avenue South
Minneapolis, MN 55419
www.jumplibrary.com

Library of Congress Cataloging-in-Publication Data

Names: Pettiford, Rebecca, author.
Title: Wind power / by Rebecca Pettiford.
Description: Minneapolis, MN: Jump!, Inc., [2016]
Series: Green planet | Audience: Ages 7-10.
Includes bibliographical references and index.
Identifiers: LCCN 2016018148 (print)
LCCN 2016018713 (ebook)
ISBN 9781620314050 (hardcover: alk. paper)
ISBN 9781624964527 (ebook)
Subjects: LCSH: Wind power—Juvenile literature.
Wind power plants—Juvenile literature.
Classification: LCC TJ820 .P48 2016 (print)
LCC TJ820 (ebook) | DDC 621.31/2136—dc23
LC record available at https://lccn.loc.gov/2016018148

Series Editor: Jenny Fretland VanVoorst
Series Designer: Anna Peterson
Book Designer: Leah Sanders
Photo Researcher: Kirsten Chang

Photo Credits: All photos by Shutterstock except: Alamy, 14, 15; Don Mammoser/Shutterstock.com, 20-21; Getty, 16-17; iStock, 12-13; Thinkstock, 1.

Printed in the United States of America at Corporate Graphics in North Mankato, Minnesota.

TABLE OF CONTENTS

CHAPTER 1

THE POWER OF WIND

People have used wind power for thousands of years. They used it to sail boats. They used it to cut wood and mill grain.

Today, we use wind power to make electricity. How? Let's find out.

The sun heats Earth's surface. It warms the air. The warm air rises. As it rises, it cools and then falls. This movement is wind.

Wind does not make **pollution**. It is a **renewable resource**. This means it will never run out. It blows whether we want it to or not. So why not use its energy to power our homes?

DID YOU KNOW?

The higher you go, the windier it is. This is why turbines are tall. More wind means more electricity.

CHAPTER 2

TURBINES AND FARMS

A **wind turbine** uses wind to make electricity. It can stand over 200 feet (61 meters) tall.

The wind turns its long blades. They can be over 100 feet (30 m) long. They can move over 200 miles (322 kilometers) per hour.

CHAPTER 9

The turning blades spin a **rotor**. The rotor connects to a **shaft**. When the shaft turns, it spins a **generator**.

This is what makes electricity. A **transformer** increases the **voltage**. Then power lines deliver it to homes and businesses.

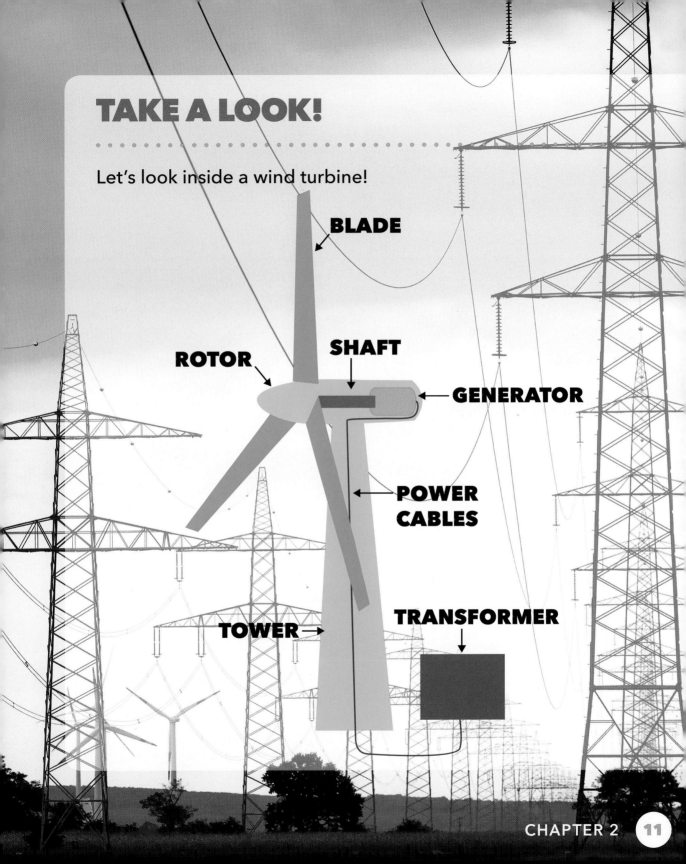

TAKE A LOOK!

Let's look inside a wind turbine!

BLADE

ROTOR

SHAFT

GENERATOR

POWER CABLES

TOWER →

TRANSFORMER

Wind farms have a lot of turbines in one place. A good place for these farms is by the coast. Many countries have **offshore** wind farms. They make more power than land wind farms. Why? Ocean winds are strong and blow all the time.

CHAPTER 3

THE FUTURE OF WIND

Many people do not like wind farms. They think they destroy the land's beauty. The blades kill thousands of bats and birds every year.

14 CHAPTER 3

Wind farms are loud. Still, as more people ask for clean energy, the number of wind farms will grow.

There will also be more small wind power operations. A home may have a small turbine on its roof. It usually gives enough power to run a few household machines.

Some tall buildings have built-in wind turbines. The World Trade Center in **Bahrain** was the first to have them.

DID YOU KNOW?

Wind power companies are working to reduce the number of animal deaths in turbines. They are trying different designs and colors. They are placing wind farms away from birds' flight paths.

Wind does not blow all the time. It is not the best way to make power. What can we do? We can combine wind and **solar power**. The sun shines during the day. The wind is stronger at night. It is also stronger in winter, when the sun is weaker. Combining solar and wind power can give us the energy we need.

Wind power is becoming more popular in every part of the world. People want clean energy. They want to save money. Wind power is one answer.

TRY THIS!

MAKE A PINWHEEL AND BLOW!

Make a pinwheel to see how wind power works. You will need the following:

- a square piece of paper
- scissors
- pencil with eraser head
- push pin

1. **Fold a corner of the paper to its opposite corner. Do the same with the next corner. Unfold the paper.**

2. **Do you see the four fold lines in the square? On each fold line, draw a pencil mark about a third of the way from the square's center. You will have four pencil marks. It should look like this:**

3. **Cut along the fold lines. Stop cutting at the pencil mark.**

4. **Bring every other corner into the center. Overlap them a little.**

5. **Stick the push pin through all four corners. The head of the pin becomes the center of the pinwheel. It sticks out on the other side. It should look like this:**

6. **Stick the sharp end of the push pin through the eraser of the pencil.**

7. **Blow air into the pockets made by the pinwheel blades. Watch it spin!**

GLOSSARY

Bahrain: A small island country in the Middle East.

generator: A machine that changes mechanical energy into electricity.

offshore: Away from the shoreline; in the sea.

pollution: Something harmful that is in the environment.

renewable resource: A supply of something in nature that is easily replaced.

rotor: A part of a machine that spins around a central point.

shaft: A bar in a machine that holds or turns other moving parts.

solar power: Power created using energy from the sun.

transformer: A device that changes the voltage of an electrical current.

voltage: The force of an electric current measured in volts.

wind farms: Areas of land with many wind turbines.

wind turbine: A tall structure with large blades attached to an engine that makes electricity.

INDEX

TO LEARN MORE

Learning more is as easy as 1, 2, 3.

1) Go to www.factsurfer.com

2) Enter "windpower" into the search box.

3) Click the "Surf" button to see a list of websites.

With factsurfer, finding more information is just a click away.